UNSPOKEN TRUTH

The Aftermath of Sexual Abuse

ALISHA WHITE

TABLE OF CONTENTS

Introduction 1

Chapter 1: Molestation 5

Chapter 2: Abandonment Issues 13

Chapter 3: Anger and Rage 21

Chapter 4: Suicidal 29

Chapter 5: Dating 41

Chapter 6: Finding a Husband 53

Chapter 7: Seeking Healing 67

Chapter 8: Learning to Forgive 81

Chapter 9: What you need to know about sexual trauma .. 91

INTRODUCTION

AT JUST ELEVEN YEARS OLD, I became a victim of sexual trauma at the hands of my favorite uncle. He was a guy that I had grown to love. He was like a best friend to me right up until he betrayed me. You see, him coming to visit me daily was normal in my life. My parents didn't even have a clue as to what would happen if I was ever left alone with him. The uncle that I cared about, so dearly taught me all about the birds and the bees long before that time should've ever come.

The trauma from what he did to me would rock my world to its core. I would go on to struggle with various issues from this single deplorable act. Anger and rage, abandonment and trust issues, even suicidal thoughts. "I" would ultimately have to learn how to fight for "me."

Learning how to forgive and heal is something that is not always an easy task to take on, but it's worth it in the end.

Whenever I think about forgiving and healing, I often think about the beautiful butterfly. "Without change, there would be no butterflies." You see, a butterfly starts as a caterpillar. Ugly, unappealing… just like my situation did with my uncle. It was nasty and ugly, and I hated being the caterpillar, I knew that I was destined to be something much greater.

So even though I went through those ups and downs, it caused me to become introspective. To examine the things that were really hindering me from becoming a butterfly. That's when I decided to allow the cocoon (that I was undoubtedly inside of at the time) to do its work. Recognizing the issues at hand is half the battle, right? As I dug deep inside myself, I realized that I didn't want to walk around in a cocoon all the time. I needed to blossom, and from there, my healing process began.

Once I decided to forgive and heal from my past is when I truly became a butterfly. Now I can spread my wings freely to fly and help someone else that may be in the caterpillar or even the cocoon stages in life. Sexual trauma is something that is not often spoken about, but it is prevalent today. It is happening to every race, sex, and religion. Statics shows that 90% of children who are abused know their abuser. A stranger abuses the other 10%. We have got to do better as a community to protect our babies from becoming another statistic. The only way we can do this is by standing up and speaking the unspoken truths about these situations.

• CHAPTER 1 •

MOLESTATION

ELEVEN-YEARS-OLD IS AN AGE when one should be hanging out with friends, jumping ropes, watching television, or just happy and relaxing with family. For the most part, I did all these things. However, there was one thing that I shouldn't have had to learn at this age, and that was sexual trauma. In December of 1992, I became a survivor of sexual trauma, an act that happened at the hands of my favorite uncle!

Every day my uncle would come to visit me NO MATTER WHAT. Day or night, he was coming to see me, and I would wait for him. He was my favorite uncle; I learned so much from him. Throughout the week, he would be at my house, helping me with my homework. I know you're probably thinking, "what's wrong with that?"

The answer to that question is that I am one of four children. Which meant there were other children there, but his attention was solely focused on me.

I was the oldest daughter, and he had his sights set on me alone. My mama and daddy had no idea that the one person that they had allowed into their home and trusted would come and wreak havoc the way he did. Not only would he be there but if he wasn't able to make it, he would call. I can remember a time when he went to jail; my mama would allow me to talk to him on the phone from prison. We wrote each other letters and each one of them ending with I love you.

I will tell you that I just thought that I was special, and I was. I was especially preyed upon, and my parents allowed this to happen. My support system failed me, and it would take nothing short of the love of God to bring me back from this mess. My support system should have been able to recognize the signs, but they didn't. They should have asked questions like, "why is he interested in ONLY her?" My uncle climbed into my little small world and gave my life meaning. He was smart, funny, and loving, which made him dangerous because no one would have ever expected him to be a predator.

No one could have ever known that the man that brought so much joy to my life would turn around and tear it down singlehandedly. I can remember one time that I hadn't seen him all that day. I waited and waited for him to come by, but he hadn't. It was a weekend night, so I begged mama to let me stay up just a little while longer, and she did. However, by eleven o'clock that night mama said, lights out. No sooner than my head hit the pillow, there he was knocking at the door.

My mama went to see who was at the door because my daddy had already left to spin records at the local club. When mama asked, "Who is it"? When he replied she turned and looked back at me standing there in my nightgown smiling. He had finally come. Mama opened the door and told him that it was late. He said he just wanted to speak before going home.

As mama stepped aside from the door, I could see him squat down as if to be on my level, I ran and jumped into his arms. He picked me up and spun me around, and as he was putting me down, he tickled me. He whispered in my ear that he would see me on tomorrow. He lived right up the street so I knew that I would. I believe that my mom should have picked up on the fact that as a niece and an uncle we were just too close.

My parents didn't see this because it should be okay for us to be as close as we were, but he was a predator. His predatory ways would cause our bond to fall completely apart. It would all come to a head the very first time I was ever left alone with him. It happened on a Thursday in December. My mama received a phone call asking if she would like to join the choir at the church we were attending.

Mama ended the conversation on the phone with a "yes!" After she hung up the phone, she began getting dressed. Mama told me that she was going to choir rehearsal, and that was it. She had never left us at home alone before, so I thought that she was joking. In my mind, if we all attended this church, we should have been allowed to go to the choir rehearsal.

A short while after mama had finished getting dressed, we heard a horn blow. Her ride had made it. I watched her grab her purse and head for the door. Although I was eleven, I was on the front porch, kicking and screaming like a two-year-old. I screamed so loud for her not to leave us, that it felt as though my tonsils were going to fall out of the back of my throat.

Instead of her coming to see what was wrong with me, she just left us there. My oldest brother was playing basketball at the school right up the street from our house. Meanwhile, me, my sister, and my baby brother were there alone. They were both looking at me as to what we would do next. I struggled to ease the tension that was happening on the front porch. I was scared out of my mind.

Then it dawned on me that we had family right up the street — my uncle. We went up the road searching for an adult to calm our fears. As we made our way past the two houses that separated our house from his, we then entered the driveway. As we climbed up on the porch of my late grandmother's house, I knocked on the door. My daddy's baby brother answered the door after explaining to him that we all were alone.

He told us to go home and that he would be there shortly. I walked away with my siblings in hand, feeling like the trip was unsuccessful, yet we did what we were told. After we had made our way back to our house, we sat on the front porch, hoping that someone would come and rescue us. We sat there on the porch in great anticipation that someone would arrive shortly. When the door swung open, we were overjoyed.

However, when I saw that it was my favorite uncle, I was able to breathe a sigh of relief. He was coming to save the day. Surely, he was going to make things better or so I thought. When he arrived on our front porch, we were so happy we went inside to the living room. Immediately, my uncle dismissed my siblings, sent them out to play on the brand-new swing set.

While they were outside playing, my uncle turned to me and asked me, "Are you a big girl or a little girl?" My reply was, "I'm a big girl, of course." I had no idea where this conversation was headed. From that point, the television screen went black. There stood my uncle in front of the chair that I was sitting in saying, let me show you what big girls are doing. He asked me to stand on the side of the chair.

From there, he pulled down my clothes, and with no hesitation, he leaned me over the arm of the chair and began kissing me between my legs. Every time I tried to get up, he would push me back further over the handle of the chair. Surely this was some horrible dream because the uncle that I loved so much wouldn't dare hurt me in such a manner. My uncle loved me, and he would never do anything to hurt me. I must be dreaming I thought, and at any moment I am going to wake up from this nightmare.

Before I knew it, I felt him release my legs and stand up, then I heard him unzipping his pants. In a moment of desperation to stop this horror I was having to endure I seized the opportunity to get away and took off running all while pulling up my pants. He was so consumed with what he was doing that he didn't even have time to reach out to me. I kept on running until the reality hit me that I had just left my two siblings alone with him back at the house. As I thought to myself, I had to go back to ensure that they were not being harmed.

I made the trip completely out of breath back towards the house. Only to find that they were still out playing on that swing set enjoying themselves. This just solidified for me that it was only me that he wanted. That's when I knew that I was going to have to help get myself out of this situation. The one thing that I hated doing was going to get my brother.

However, if there ever was a time that I needed him, it was now. So, off I went to go and get my brother from the school. Him and his friends were there shooting basketball. They were all so upset about him having to leave in the middle of the game, but I couldn't care about that. I was fighting for my life. I needed him more than anything at that moment. I didn't want to disclose to him what had happened in front of his friends.

So, I told him that mama sent me to come and get him because she had to leave. Even to him, that didn't seem right, and therefore he knew that it must have been serious. He wanted to know where the other kids were, and I told him that I had to leave them. The more I talked, the more questions he had. I could tell that he was trying to make it make sense. In this case, there was nothing that was going to make any sense. My uncle, my favorite uncle, had just violated me in the most horrible way imaginable.

• CHAPTER 2 •

ABANDONMENT ISSUES

MY OLDEST BROTHER AND I arrived at the house only to find him still there. My brother walked in and went straight to my mama's room for her gun. When he came back into the living room, he told my uncle that he needed to leave right then and there. Afterward, I contacted my aunt, who was living in Baton Rouge at the time, which was just a little under thirty minutes away from Zachary, where we lived. She said to me that I was to stay exactly where I was because I needed to go to the hospital.

She also told me not to bathe nor use the restroom at all. As I sat there waiting for her to come and take me to the hospital, everything in me wanted to wipe the saliva that was on me, OFF. I felt nasty. I was disgusted with the very thought of what had just happened. A short while later my aunt came, she told my brother to lock up the house and to let no one in. She also told him that he needed to inform my parents once they got home where we were.

From there, we headed to Lane Memorial Hospital. Once we got there, my aunt walked up to the window and told the person at the desk that she needed to check me in. They asked her what we were there for, and of course, she says, "She's been raped" right there in the lobby. From that point on, I felt like everyone that was whispering was talking about me. I sat there and tried to pretend that I was paying close attention to the television.

My aunt kept asking me if I was alright. I had just been violated by one of my most favorite people in the world. I was not alright! Yet! My response was, "I'm alright." Once they called my name, and we went to the back, the nurse instructed me to remove my clothes and put on a gown. As if I needed them prodding down there anymore today, I thought to myself.

They immediately began their testing by asking questions that I hated answering. The more personal the questions were, the more embarrassed I was. I didn't know how to answer the questions without becoming flushed. There I was at a hospital without either of my parents going through one of the most embarrassing times of my life. After getting through the process of telling my story to my aunt, the nurse, and the doctor, I wanted to ball up and just die.

I wanted nothing more than for them to all to leave me alone because the people that I needed the most were nowhere to be found. The clock on the wall of the hospital room that I was in made sure that I knew just how long I had been going through the process. It had been hours! Hours of them asking question after question. Hours of them swabbing me in places where the sun never shines. Hours of me there without one of the parents that God had given authority over me.

I was mortified, I had no clue what to do next, so I just sat there looking off into space — praying to God that He would speed up the process and make all this stuff go away. My daddy was the first of my parents to show up. The look in his eye told me that his heart had been broken into pieces. I wanted to run to him and bury my head in his chest and just cry. For some odd reason, I knew that if I had done so, he would have probably lost it all right there.

As he walked closer toward the side of the bed that I was in, he put his hand on my shoulder. The room was completely silent for the moment. Daddy finally broke the silence by asking me what happened. There I was having to repeat this story again. I wanted to tell him that I told that story already, and I wasn't going to say it again. I wanted to scream at him what took you so long to get here. I wanted to yell that I was tore up to pieces about all of this. Instead, I just told the story once more.

Right before being discharged from the hospital, mama arrived. Immediately I thought to myself that I was done telling the story, but oddly enough, she didn't ask. Her not asking, hurt me just as much as her leaving us alone. It spoke to my little mind and heart and said that she didn't care. When my aunt saw that mama had made it, she felt like it would be alright now that my mama was there. She couldn't have been farther from the truth.

As she began saying her goodbyes, when she got to me, she looked me in the eyes and said to me that if I ever needed her that I could call. I wished that mama would have been taking notes, but something told me that she wasn't. As we left the hospital mama insisted that I ride with her. I thought that maybe on the ride home, she would apologize to me, but she did no such thing. The ride home was completely silent; no one said anything; we just let the radio play.

When we arrived home, all eyes were on me to see if I was alright. I hated that more than anything. I was fine, physically anyway. However, I played it cool, but I was ripped to shreds on the inside. What was going on inside of me was something that my eleven-year-old self couldn't put into words. I wished that my mama knew enough about me to investigate my soul and say you are not alright.

Even if she didn't know how to help me, her acknowledging my feelings would have made me feel better. Instead I went off to take myself a good old hot bath. Before heading to take my bath, mama stopped me in the hallway. She asked, "Are you alright?" I wanted to say to her HELL NO, I was indeed "not" alright. The uncle that understood me, encouraged me enough to make sure that my voice was heard, turned out to be the same uncle that walked into my living room, and walked out with my innocence.

I was never getting that back, and I was mad as hell about it. So, no, I was definitely not alright. I was made to stay home with no guidance and no direction as to what I should do next. I was mad as hell, and the more I thought about it, the angrier I became. I was left alone to wallow in the very thought of being left alone. Still, I answered and told her that I was okay.

I said that I was okay because what else could I have said. "Mama, are you stupid for leaving me??" or "Mama, you left me, and this is what happened!" maybe I should have said, "Mama, this is all your fault." The reality of this is everyone knew that she had left me.

She didn't even look back as the car went up the street away from the house. All my screaming, crying, and jumping up and down went unnoticed. The reaction of her being unemotionally aware told me that she didn't even care, she couldn't. She never sat me down to say, "Daughter, I love you" or "I am so sorry that this happened to you" not even "I am here if you want to talk." In retrospect, nothing about that day said to me that she felt bad about her decision to leave me alone.

• CHAPTER 3 •

ANGER AND RAGE

AFTER THE MOLESTATION, I was still made to go to school and in a small town where everyone knew everyone. This was horrific for me because if my parents didn't talk to me about being molested, then you know that I was not prepared to answer the questions that were to come. Teachers asked, and so did the students, and I had no idea what to say. I had to suppress all my feelings and emotions. Fighting to keep the anger and rage I felt inside from spilling out in front of others.

The kids were relentless, constantly asking what happened. I kept avoiding the questions until finally, I heard someone say, "She must have liked it." That's when the emotional rollercoaster that I had been on came to a screeching halt. I jumped out of my seat because I recognized the little boy that said it. I ran towards him, but the teacher stopped me before I ever reached his desk. All I know is that I saw red. I didn't realize what had happened until they tried to get me to calm down in the front office.

A short while later, my parents decided that we were going to make the move to the city of Baton Rouge. I just knew that the change of scenery would be good for my family and me. Boy, was I wrong! I mean, it was anything but good for the family and especially for me. Me and daddy were very close, and I was his first baby girl.

Our bond couldn't have been any closer, even though daddy wasn't big on words his actions spoke to me. Daddy also was the one that protected me from mama. For some odd reason, I could never do anything right in her eyes. After the move, mama and daddy's marriage seemed to be falling apart. They didn't communicate the way they had once been able to, and it seemed as though they hated one another.

Eventually, they got a divorce, and it felt like he divorced me too. I was scared to live in the house with mama without any protection. My heart shattered into pieces the day I came home and found daddy packing.

He was leaving us. He was leaving "me." I didn't know how to deal with that. It made me resent mama even more now than ever.

The week before daddy had been thrown out of the house, he had taken us to the doctor while mama was at work. When we arrived, we sat and waited to be called to come to the back. That day my older brother almost ran out of the doctor's office because he didn't want any shots. While they were tending to him, the nurse asked me to give a urine sample in a cup. I went into the bathroom and I wiped just as the nurse had asked me to, and I collected the urine specimen in the cup.

Once I brought it to her, she asked my daddy had I started my menstrual cycle. Daddy could have just fainted right there in the room. Before I knew it, he told the nurse to ask me. I responded and told her that I had not. As the visit was coming to an end the doctor asked to speak with daddy privately.

I overheard him tell him that my menstrual cycle was going to be starting soon because they saw traces of blood in my urine. Daddy came out of the room to ask, "Who wants to go to McDonald's?" We all said,

"Meeeee!" of course. So, from the doctor to the restaurant to home. When mama came in from work, I overheard daddy telling her what had happened at the doctor. Two days would go by before I got the first sign of cramps at school.

After going to the bathroom, I realized that it had, in fact, came on. I went to the office to call my mama. She answered the phone with a soft "Hello?" I responded with, "Ma, I need to come home." her reply was, "Why?" and I told her that my stomach was hurting. She told me that I would be fine. As I hung up the phone, I felt as though I needed to do something fast. So, I did what I knew to do, and that was to run for help.

Once again, no help from her, so when I found out that daddy was leaving me, I was furious. Eventually, one of my aunts helped me out with my cycle issue. I knew that day that I was going to be in big trouble without him. There I was without my daddy there to protect me, and that made me angry. Weeks had gone by, and I was barely getting by with just mama.

I mostly tried to stay out of her way all the time. This one day, I raised my hand at school to ask to go to the restroom. Once I got in there, I saw some girls in there smoking weed and cutting class. This was exciting to me because in Zachary, we never did anything like this. As a matter of fact, I didn't know what it was. I watched those girls pass that perfectly rolled blunt around and when it reached me, I was too scared to hit it.

Just as I was about to walk out of the restroom the principal came in. He escorted us all out of the bathroom and to the office. I tried my hardest to explain that I hadn't been smoking, and I was there to use the restroom. I showed him my hall pass and everything. Still he called my mama. The words on the other end of that phone were like a rocket blowing up my ear canal. She said, "When you get home, I'm gone beat your a**!" Nothing more and nothing less. I was right; she just didn't want to believe me.

The day zoomed by, and finally, I was out of school only to return to a danger zone. As I walked home, I told myself that today was going to be the day. I was just going to have to hit her back. I refused to get beat on for nothing. I don't know why, but I said it out of my mouth, and my ears heard it. The entire walk home I was practicing boxing moves. Little did I know that it wouldn't turn out as I thought. I guess I hadn't thought about mama hitting me back at all, that never crossed my mind at all.

So, I made it home only to find mama sitting in her chair waiting on me. I walked past her as if I didn't see her, which ultimately made her mad. When she called me, I knew that it was on. I looked in the mirror and said to myself, "You got this." I went to see what she wanted, I stood there while she hollered at me. The whole time I said nothing, I just stood there.

She yelled at me that since I was suspended for a week, I was going to be working for a week. She concluded the conversation by telling me that I needed to start with hanging out the clothes on the line. As I stood on the back porch and looked at the tall grass that came above my hip line, I said to myself this is for the birds. I came up with a plan that I needed to just run away. Which I did, I made it safe and sound to my cousin's house.

I wanted so badly to tell mama what was on my mind. So, I dialed *69 and her number. I cussed her out so bad on that line. I told her everything that I ever thought about her and then some, and then I hung up. I wanted her to know everything so every time I thought about something else, I just called her and told her some more of my shenanigans.

I told her that if she ever thought about putting her hands on me that she would regret it. I told her how I owed her for all the times she beat my butt for absolutely nothing at all. I told her that I couldn't wait to see her so that I could slap the taste out of her mouth like she had done me so many times before. My cousins and I had a great laugh at what I told mama. However, one of them betrayed me by calling her to tell her where I was.

By the end of the night, my mama and two of her sisters made the trip to come get me. However, they knew that they wouldn't just get me to come out and get in the van with them, so they sent one of my cousins in to get me. He walked me outside onto the balcony and down the stairs from my cousin's house. I was kicking and screaming because mama was sitting in the back of my aunt's van. That's when I knew that I was going to have to back up everything that I had ever said on that phone.

As soon as my cousin put me in the van I started swinging. Mama picked me up and threw my head up against the window. I just knew that I was going out into oncoming traffic. When my head hit that glass window, it felt like it shut down my whole body. I just fell to the floor, and then mama started kicking me. I knew then that I was getting ready to die right then and there on the floor.

So, I did what I knew best to do and that was bite her ankle. That gave me time to catch my breath at least. I then mustered up the strength to pull myself up from the floor. I began swinging, and the fight continued until my aunt came and got me and I sat in the back of the van with her. Once we made it home mama opened the front door and I ran through the house and out the back door. I heard mama holler, "She's going out the back!" and then my aunt rounded the corner.

When I saw her standing there with a chain in her hand, I thought that I was going to have fight yet again. I prepared myself for the fight, but my aunt was cool. She threw down her chain as if to say I come in peace. She also talked me into staying there with my mama. That night mama slept in her recliner chair in the living room, in fear that I might run again.

• CHAPTER 4 •

SUICIDAL

THE FUSSING AND FIGHTING with mama would continue for what felt like a lifetime. By the time I was in high school, life for me didn't look promising. Being so filled with anger and rage kept me in a lot of trouble. Either I was getting suspended for fighting or for not doing what an adult told me to do. For me, adults never understood me, or maybe I didn't understand them. However, my adolescent mind wouldn't allow me to grasp why adults and I never got along.

The pain was so real in my mind that it made it hard to focus sometimes. The anger from the molestation and the fact that mama left me alone after she heard me screaming and hollering for her tainted the mental picture of what an adult was supposed to look like to me.

The molestation would haunt me for a very long time. It got to the point that I wasn't sleeping or eating, and that made me irritable and difficult to be around. Being sleep deprived will cause you to lose a grip on the important things in life. All the pain in my head and my heart made it hard for me to focus, so I started drinking.

Mad dog 20/20, was a very popular drink in that day. They called it mad dog because after consuming it, you acted like a literal mad dog, at least I did. Every time I was intoxicated from this drink, it made me want to fight more. When I didn't have any alcoholic beverages to numb the pain, I was sleeping because I was high off Nyquil. Nyquil was a source of alcohol that mama always had on hand in the medicine cabinet. Because she had four kids, she would always buy the double pack. One stayed in the cabinet and the other one under my pillow, which no one ever knew about.

I was used to having long days at school. My peers didn't understand me, and most times, I felt like an out-cast. The molestation altered my perspective on life, and others couldn't understand unless they had experienced it personally. Depression had a grip on my soul, and it was-n't letting me go. Those school days were mentally draining and caused me to be unable to deal with anything else in life. The aftermath of sexual abuse had me in bondage. My peace, joy, and happiness were nowhere to be found.

One day after school, I came home to an empty house. On this day there was no alcohol or Nyquil. I needed something to mask my pain, so I decided that I was going to kill myself. The torment was too much to bear, and I wanted to end it all. I needed to get away from all the pain and just be free. I called my friends to tell them that they wouldn't be seeing me the next day at school. I figured no one would miss me anyway.

I went to the medicine cabinet to find some pills to take. I wanted something that would put me to sleep so I could die peacefully. However, the handful of Tylenol that I took made me sleepy and my stomach hurt like hell. That night my friends called all night long to check on me; it wasn't until I started crying that they knew something was wrong. By the end of the night, I lay in my bed groggy from the pills and trying to fall asleep. This wasn't going according to plan.

One of my friends was able to get in touch with my mama. After she told her what I had done, my mama stated that she would take care of it. After hanging up the phone, she went on to doing something else. I fought through all that night trying to make myself throw up; I really didn't want to die. I just wanted the pain from what was done to me to be over. I wanted the pain from my mama, not putting her arms around me and saying to me, "I love you." I just wanted the pain to go away so that I could be free.

I wanted to know how it felt to be happy. Every day, I woke up and wanted to die. I just wanted the freedom to be happy again. I didn't think that I was ever going to get that back. I wanted my life back. I wanted my laugh, my smile, and my innocence back, but I was never going to get that. I vowed that I would never let anyone else hurt me in such a way again.

When I woke up the next morning, I was still groggy. My stomach was still hurting, but I made it my business to go to school. I didn't want my friends to think that I was dead when I wasn't. When I got there, just to drink water made me vomit. I was nauseous and sleepy all day long. Mama hadn't even bothered to check on her daughter that morning. She just got up and went to work as usual.

Thankfully, my aunt called the school to check on me. She was informed that I had been sleeping all day. She called my mama at work and told her that I needed to go to the hospital. Mama was livid and said that she was missing money messing around with me. She was not happy at all, but she came and took me to the hospital.

Once we made it there, she told the doctors that they needed to lock me up because I was crazy. Once the doctor found out that this wasn't my first time trying to commit suicide, he became afraid. He told me the story about a girl that they had just rolled down to the morgue right before I came in. Her parents had brought her in the night before because she had tried to commit suicide. They pumped her stomach and sent her home. The parents brought her back again that morning, and this time they were too late.

He decided that he was going to pump my stomach and send me out to an institution. Mama had finally gotten her wish, which was to have me locked up. I was so afraid of what that looked like for me. I'd heard so many horror stories about people being raped and beaten in jail. A mental institution in my mind was the same thing, being locked up, doing what other people tell you to do.

I felt that same sense of loneliness, unworthiness, and abandonment. Mama had no idea what she was doing to me. She had no idea that she was trying to fix something in the natural, but my problem was spiritual. The help that I needed could only come from God Himself, but you don't know what you don't know, right?

The team of doctors and nurses returned to my room; they all held me down while forcing a tube down my throat. They pumped my stomach with activated charcoal. Afterward, the doctor told my mama to just hold tight that he had ordered the Acadian Ambulance to come and transfer me to a local mental health center. While I must admit that I needed some help, this wasn't it.

By the time the ambulance arrived, I had worried myself sick about the ride. I was still throwing up all of what they hadn't pumped out of me. I begged my mama to make sure that she stayed behind the ambulance. She assured me that she would. As the two male paramedics loaded me up into the ambulance, I tried to calm my nerves when I saw mama car right behind the ambulance. The paramedics made small talk because they knew that I was nervous.

After they had me safe and secure, one of them took a glance at the paperwork from the hospital. It read that I was to be transported to Margaret Dumas Mental Health Center. I initiated a conversation with the paramedics and convinced them that the paperwork was wrong. One of the paramedics made the trip inside to see if the paperwork was correct, and they assured him that it was.

As they were preparing to leave with me out of the parking lot, I heard them hit the siren as if he was saying that he had precious cargo in the back. The other paramedic talked with me the entire way. I kept my eyes glued on mama car as I could see her outside the small windows on the back. She was doing good until midways there, and then I saw her turn off. Alone again, I thought, every time I thought maybe she loves me, she found some way to show me that wasn't true.

As I laid on the stretcher, I silently cried a little because I had no one. No one was there for me to hold my hand or tell me that they loved me. That was the one thing that I wanted more than anything, and that was to be loved. By the time we made it to the mental health center, they had rolled me out and into the facility. Once inside, they said that I could climb off the stretcher. They handed my paperwork to the lady at the front counter, and they said their goodbyes.

A short while later a lady came out to get me, and she asked was there anyone there with me. I immediately told her no, because mama wasn't there. The lady walked me back into her office, and we began talking about what had brought me in. After just a few rounds of questioning, she told me that I could have a seat out in the foyer to wait for my ride. The lady didn't think that I was crazy, and nor did I need to be there.

A few minutes had gone by, and mama came into the facility and found me sitting there. I wanted to jump on her in the facility but didn't want to risk getting into any trouble. Mama became upset when the lady explained to her that I was just depressed. She wrote me out a prescription for Prozac and sent us on our way.

After the day I had, I contemplated suicide even more so. I just wanted to be away from mama, she didn't like me, and I was starting to feel that I shared her sentiment. The ride home was that of complete silence with just the music playing. It was déjà vu all over again for me. Little did I know that life was about to take a turn for the better.

On the ride home, I knew what I had to do. I needed to kill myself and be done with it. However, when I arrived home, I found a box in the mailbox addressed to me. Who would be sending me something, I thought? I immediately began opening the box, and to my surprise, there were several CDs inside. Then I remembered the card that had come in the mail about several CDs for a penny.

After I made my selection on the card, I stuffed a penny in the envelope and sent it off. Honestly, I thought they were just going to take my penny and never send me anything. Yet there I was with this box filled with CDs. Among the CDs in the box was Yolanda Adams and Bebe & CeCe Winans, just to name a few.

I took my CDs into the den to listen to them that day. I ended up crying out to God after listening to Yolanda Adams's album titled "The Essential." I listened to that album day and night crying out to God, and I felt His presence enter my house that day. That night God visited me in my dream to tell me that joy comes in the morning. I knew then that if I had died the night before, I would never have been able to experience the joy that God had for me. I knew that I needed to do something different if I wanted different results.

Hebrews 11:6 says, "And it is impossible to please God without faith. Anyone who wants to come to Him must believe that God exists and that He rewards those who sincerely seek Him." I knew that I needed to seek God in every aspect of my life. I had to make up my mind that I was going to be fully committed and submitted in my own healing. I had learned how to fight and that was something that I had done well.

However, it was time to fight for my healing, deliverance, my peace, my joy, and my understanding. I needed to open my eyes to see that the enemy had been plotting on my demise since I was eleven. I had to stand up and take back everything that he took from me. The Bible tells us in John 10:10 says that the enemy comes to steal, kill and to destroy. But Jesus says that I have come that they may have life, and they may have it more abundantly.

I decided that the enemy couldn't have my peace, my joy, and he, for sure, couldn't have my life. That wouldn't stop him from trying, though, but what I have learned now is that whenever the enemy is attacking me hard, that means he has peeked inside of my future, and he knows that it gets greater later.

• CHAPTER 5 •

DATING

DATING WOULDN'T COME EASY for me. I mean, how could I try to date when I was so messed up? The molestation kept its grips on my soul and made it hard for me to give my heart away to anyone. Seclusion is something that I felt like I needed, and so for my eighteenth birthday, I moved out of my mama's house.

I had made mention to mama that I would be moving out, but she said nothing. On the day of my move, she didn't have much to say. I had been moving all that day, and on my last trip to my apartment, my car broke down. My landline hadn't been connected, so I had to walk up the street to use the payphone. Once there, I called mama to ask her if she would come and take me to get something to eat because my car had broken down.

Her response was, "You are playing big girl now; figure it out." I really and truly thought that she was playing with me, but she wasn't. I called her once more only to get the same answer, so I decided that I needed to reach out to someone else. By the end of the night, I had eaten, bathed, and was in bed watching television.

As I lay there in my bed, all I could think of was that I was at peace. I had just made a move on my own, and because I was eighteen, I had landed a job at a local convenience store. I was on track to getting my happiness back, and I wasn't willing to let it go for anybody. Little did I know that mama was struggling to try to come to grips of her child moving out on her own. Even though she never verbalized to me that it hurt her feelings, I knew it did.

Deciding to move out was for me and not her. So, I kept the line moving in the right direction for me. I worked the night shift at my job. I loved it because that meant that I was working by myself and no one else. Just the way I liked things to be. At the store, I would see guys come and go.

I had my fair share of dating invitations. I will tell you that I was terrified of getting into a relationship. I mainly kept guys at bay, so that no one would have to know my secret. I had no earthly reason for calling what was done to me, my secret, but that's how I felt. I felt as though I was a victim, and every time I thought about it, I was being victimized all over again.

I wanted to move past the pain, shame, and the hurt of it all, but how? Since the move, I was learning how to do things differently. I knew how to move and do things alone because I wasn't going to hurt me. I decided to keep my options open though just in cased Mr. Right came along.

One night while at work, I received a phone call from a gentleman who was interested in me. While I only chatted with him for a few minutes over the phone, he made mention of how beautiful my feet were. For me, that was something different, and even though he hadn't asked to date me, he and I became friends. He was so charming, and we eventually found ourselves spending a lot of time together. Because of my insecurities, I would take long breaks from him, just to protect myself.

I had to make sure that he was in this thing just for me. I kept him away from my family and friends because I had no clue as to if we were going to make it. Two years had gone by before I had ever invited anyone to my apartment. It was my safety net, and I wasn't willing to give it away. However, he had shown me that he was willing to be there just for me. So, I thought it would be okay to introduce him to the family.

One day my siblings called me and asked me to take them to the state fair. As I told them that I would, I ran it by him to see if that was something that he wanted to do. That night we took my siblings to the state fair. After leaving the fair and picking up something for them to eat, I went to drop them off. He and I then went back to my apartment. My heart was beating so fast that I felt as though I was going to pass out.

I needed something to take the edge off before I could think about getting through the night. The whole ride home, I couldn't stop smiling because I knew that my siblings were happy. That meant a lot to me, and so I thought it would be fine to allow him over. Once we got back to my apartment, I knew that I had intentionally made sure not to put myself in a position where I would be forced to do something I didn't want to do.

However, this was different; he had passed all the tests that I had given him. Against my better judgment, I decided that this would be the night that I would lose my virginity. So, once inside the apartment, we decided to let the smoke from the blunts fill the air. All while sipping on gin and juice, it gave me all the courage I needed to go all the way. That night I gave away my virginity, and I also conceived my oldest daughter.

How could I be so stupid to have premarital sex without any protection? I knew better, but the alcohol mixed with herbs rolled up in that brown cigar made me throw my inhibitions to the wind. Afterward, he immediately looked me in the eye and said, "You know you're pregnant, right?" I couldn't believe that I could possibly be pregnant. I wasn't ready for a child. I was still trying to figure out who I was, along with who was the guy in my bed, undressing me so casually.

Before going to bed, I put it out of my head about the pregnancy scare. I thought no more about until his mother saw me and told me that I was pregnant. She claimed that my breast was filling out and so I knew that I needed to make an appointment. On the day of my appointment, one of my aunts called to check on me. She could hear him in the background, and she asked me why he wasn't at work. I told her that he was going to drive me to my doctor's appointment. She didn't say much after that, and we hung up the phone.

Before I could get back into my apartment from the doctor's appointment, I could hear the phone ringing. I rushed inside to pick up the phone, and it was my aunt calling to ask, "What are we having?" I told her that I didn't know yet and that I was only a few weeks pregnant. The scream she let out was heart-piercing, she finally calmed down long enough to tell me how proud my grandmother would be if she could see me. I felt like everything was going to be alright. I just knew that my mama would share in the happiness that my aunt and I did.

After getting off the phone with my aunt, I called to tell my mama. She said, "I do not want you to call or bring that ugly a** baby of yours to my house." I was crushed; I had no idea what I was going to do without her. I know that I had laid down and made the baby, but I was scared. For the next eight months, I cried every day because I was yet again alone. I could never understand why I felt like a motherless child when I had a mother.

Because of the feeling of being alone again, I became a little more withdrawn from everyone. Around my eighth-month mama decided to call to see If I had my baby. I hated the emotional rollercoaster that she would put me through, but because I felt as though I needed her, I just said "no." In 2001, we welcomed a beautiful baby girl into the world. She would be the first grandchild on both sides of our families.

At the end of 2002, we found out that we would be expanding our family with another baby. He came in 2003, he was so handsome, and I wanted nothing but the best for them both. At the beginning of this relationship, we were the best of friends; we did everything together. When the kids came along, he began wanting to go out alone. You see, motherhood had matured me in ways that I never thought possible. I had no desire to hang out, smoke weed, and drink alcohol all day.

Instead, I spent my days working, sterilizing baby bottles, changing diapers, feeding kids, and teaching them new things. I was completely head over heels in love with my babies, but the fact that he wasn't as committed as I was caused a breakdown in the relationship. By the time the babies started coming, I had started a new career working with people with mental disabilities. I loved being needed, and I was able to give of myself to them in a way that I couldn't have ever imagined. While I was out finding myself by working in this new field, my relationship was falling apart right before my eyes.

One day I received a phone called for my children's father accusing me of cheating on him. I had no idea where that was coming from at all, the guy that he accused me of didn't even know my name. After getting off the phone with him, one of my coworkers, who was much older than I was at the time, told me that he was cheating. Since I was at work, I didn't allow myself to think much about the issue, but I was going to address it at home.

By the time I made it home, I had walked straight into the house and went to the bathroom to start my bathwater. This was something that I had done daily after working in a group home; I didn't want to pass germs on to my kids. For some reason, this day would be very different from the others. Once I got out of the bath, I went to the kitchen to get dinner started. While in the kitchen, he walked up behind me, and I felt something hard and cold-pressed up against my head.

He told me that if he found out that I was cheating that he was going to blow my head off. As I stood there, I knew that this relationship had run its course. The next day I went downtown to file a restraining order against him. This kept him away for a while, but because of the history that we had we found ourselves together once again.

In 2004, we decided that we would try to put our differences aside to focus on our babies. The fourth of July was approaching, and he decided that he would make plans for us to be together. He took us shopping and out to eat, and that day turned out perfect. The next day on the fourth of July, I got up that morning and prepared breakfast, and afterward, I'd asked him to take out the trash. I had the music blasting as I listen to some smooth R&B while cleaning.

I realized that it was taking him a while to come back into the house. So, I walked down the walkway looking for him. I ended up looking into the hallway of the other apartment building. There I found him smoking a blunt with about four females in the hallway. That was it for me. I was done with all the madness, and I was not going to allow him to make a fool out of me.

So, I went back into my apartment and locked my door but was unaware that he had left the den window unlocked. I looked up, and he was standing in the kitchen, ripping up all the clothes that he had bought for us. Also, he was calling me out of my name. I begged him to stop, but he didn't, and so I pulled out the very same gun that he had put against my head, and I shot him.

I wasn't aware that I could even go to such a dark place, but here I was. Standing there, holding a gun that I never heard go off and watching him scream in agony on the floor. Yet he still managed to call me more names, and I proceeded to cock the gun again. From there, he picked himself up and ran out of the apartment.

Later, the police would arrive to find me standing there with my protection order. I only had to go down to the police station to give a written statement of what happened. For the rest of the day, my babies and I enjoyed our day with family, but my mind never left the pain that

I had caused him. By the end of the night, I would be adding the nightmares of people coming after me to kill me for shooting him to my already drama-filled night. That night I was going to need major drugs to soothe the pain that was in my heart.

• CHAPTER 6 •

FINDING A HUSBAND

RIGHT AFTER ALL THE CHAOS that happened with the kids' dad, I was very guarded when it came to another man being a part of my life. I eventually moved out of the apartment, where I had shot the Father of my kids. I just wanted a fresh start for the kids and me. I moved a little closer to home so that I could have help with the kids. I also applied for another job working as a mental health tech in a mentally disabled group home.

When I was hired, they only had fifteen hours a week to offer me, but I took it anyway. Being in this field had its rewards, I loved the fact that I was able to be there for others. Shortly after working, I was rewarded for taking the initiative to update all the client's programs there. Working with people with mental disabilities came naturally to me; it was something that I loved. Working with those individuals made me forget all about the issues that had plagued me years before. Also, working with them was a great escape from all I had going on at home.

While there, I started praying and worshipping God regularly. Although I worked every Sunday, inside of my apartment, you could feel the presence of God because me and the kids worshipped daily. Although I wanted to be loved and to have someone that only had eyes for me, I knew that I wasn't ready to put myself back on the market so soon. Not because I thought that I was getting back with their Father but because of the dark place that I found myself in scared me. I didn't know that I had that in me, I guess from years of taking crap from other people.

Having to suppress my feelings had really gotten the best of me. So, for the time being, I set out to be the best mother that I could be. Christmas time came, and we were all in the holiday spirit at the group home. They even gave us a bonus which was unheard of at a group home. I decided that we should go shopping.

We went to a store called "Gators." Gators was a store that sold pretty much everything, and I was there to take advantage of the low prices they had. I was browsing down the aisle, I looked up, and I ended up making eye contact with this guy that was there purchasing snacks. As I looked away, I kept saying to myself, "Please don't let him come over here." However, he came and followed me down the aisle while I shopped.

He finally got the courage to say, "You look like a nice young lady, can I have your phone number?" I told him that he didn't want to be bothered with me, and he asked me why? I responded with "because I have seven kids," he then said that he loved kids. I realized that he wasn't going to give up and so I told him to give me his number, which he did. I really didn't have any plans on calling this dude.

He wasn't ugly, but he didn't meet at least five things that was on my list. You know the list that we make up in our minds like light skin or dark skin, height, weight, hair, appearance, and sometimes money, etc. He didn't meet the list, and therefore I had no plans on calling him. I only told him that because I wanted to shop in peace.

Sometime had gone by after I met him, and while I didn't like him, I hadn't thrown away his number. One day while sitting at work, I decided to clean out my purse, and that when I ran across his phone number. I decided that months had gone by, and he might have forgotten all about me. However, I wanted nothing more than just a friendship. He really wanted to have a relationship, but he didn't pressure me into it. We found ourselves spending a lot of time on the phone together.

Morning, noon, and night we were talking, and it felt good to have someone to talk to you that wasn't about getting into your bed. However, I didn't want to continue spending any more of my time with this guy. I wanted the guy that God had for me. I wanted my "Mr. Right"! One day, as I was leaving work, a coworker asked me if I had plans for the evening. That's when it dawned on me that I had nothing to do and no one to see.

I was on my way home to a lonely apartment to take a bath, eat, and watch television before falling asleep. I must admit that this guy was pursuing me hard, but the more he pursued me, the more I pulled away. Against my better judgment, I decided that I would give him a try to see how he was in person. So, I invited him over to my apartment the next day to watch movies and eat pizza. I had everything ready to go when he came over as soon as he walked in, he was asking about my kids.

My kids were with my mama because it was okay for me to mess up my life, but I, for sure, wasn't going to take them on the ride. Besides, I wasn't sure where the relationship was going. I wasn't going to bring my kids around before I knew what I was dealing with. A year would go by before he could meet them. However, this guy was so sweet to me because every payday he would swing by and slide money under my door.

He didn't ask if I needed it or not, I had kids, and therefore he figured I needed money. I had never in my life had a man to go out of his way to give me money. I didn't know how to handle it, and so I went into my closet and pulled down a shoebox. I put all the money that he had given me in that box. I just didn't want him saying that I owed him anything in return.

He was going out of his way to make sure that we were good, and it was nice. However, because I was so independent, I really didn't like it when he did things like spending money on us. Yet and still, he kept on surprising me. For instance, one day, I pulled up to the daycare to pick up my kids, and to pay their fees. Only to find out that a handsome gentleman had been over there to pay their fees already. All I could think was, he didn't even know who my kids were because I had never introduced them to him.

I was very cautious about who the kids were going to be around. Even though he was doing all of this for me and the kids, I was still praying for my "Mr. Right," and every time I prayed, he would call. I really and truly did not feel like this man was my husband. I fought it tooth and nail. As I became closer to God and still praying for my "Mr. Right," I knew that my time was going to come. So, I stayed faithful to the Father every day.

Praise and worship was something that I had to do, along with reading my Bible. Going to church and checking it off my list of things to do meant nothing to me. I knew that I had to have a relationship with the Father, and not just religion as usual. You see, religion is where you go to church and "act" Holy, but relationship is when you know the Father and the Father knows you. It's just like everyone wants money, but they don't want to work for it.

Just like everyone wants to go to Heaven, but not everyone is willing to give up the things of the world to make it there. I knew that I was going to have to take my own advice. I was going to have to do the work and allow God to bless me as only He could. I knew that I needed Him more than anything, and I was determined to have Him in my life. As for my husband, I was willing to wait a lifetime for him because I knew that God wouldn't send me just anybody.

I knew that I was destined to be someone's wife, but whose is what was unknown. The more this guy pursued me, the more, I kept denying what was right before my very eyes. I can remember one day he called me, and for some odd reason, his voice aggravated me. So, I said to him, look, I'm sorry, but this isn't going to work because I am no longer doing worldly guys. I had to tell him that I was waiting for God to send me a godly man, and I hung up the phone. He didn't call me back that day.

In fact, it would be a week before I heard from him. It was on a Sunday evening when he called, and I was at work. He asked, "Guess what I did today?" and I said, "what? He said, "I went to church." Next Sunday, I am getting baptized and would love it if you could make it, he said.

I was floored. I couldn't believe that he had done such a thing. Although I couldn't make his baptism because of work, it was nice to see him take a leap of faith. However, my flesh still wasn't convinced that he was the one. God was going to have to sit me down and tell me straight up that this was my husband.

A few weeks later, my supervisor said in a staff meeting that we were getting ready to update our employee files. That meant background checks and driving history to be verified again. That's when it dawned on me that I failed to go to court after everything had happened with the kids' father. This resulted in a bench warrant being issued for my arrest. So, the next day or so I took off and went to the courthouse to clear my name.

I sat there waiting to be called up to the podium to speak to the judge. All the individuals that had gone before me were there to get their bench warrants recalled. However, when she got to my name, she held me contempt of court for thirty days. I was the only female that day to leave the courthouse on the paddy wagon. As I sat there the only thing that separated me from the male offenders was a see-through gate. I had never felt like such a piece of meat before this day.

They were all barking at me as if I was the only girl in the world. I tried hard to ignore them, but that's kind of a challenge when they are right up in your face. All I kept thinking was that I had to spend an entire month I spent away from my babies. The change of events that happened in that jail cell would change my life forever. For one, I knew that orange was a very cute color on me, but prison orange was not something that I wanted to wake up to daily.

For two, I watched another lady try to cut her own neck with a razor blade over another woman. Then there was this older lady that had been in there a while. She knew everything about everyone, and she had set her sights on me. I can still remember how I felt when she told me that I was on the top bunk looking down on everyone else as if I wasn't in prison too. Truthfully speaking, I didn't think that I was better than anyone in prison.

Those thoughts never crossed my mind, but what I was thinking was how could so many of us end up in there from all different walks of life. For me, it was mind-boggling as I was trying to make sense of it all. The ladies in there looked like normal people that just made a simple mistake in life. By the end of the night, I had begun making friends, and we ended up talking about relationships. As everyone went around the room and shared their own experience, it soon became my turn.

I spoke about how I had been praying to God asking him for my "Mr. Right." I also told them that God hadn't sent him yet. The older lady response messed me all the way up. She asked me if you asked God for a million dollars in a red purse, but He gave you a million dollars in a black bag, would you not take the money? I had never been speechless before, but I was that day.

How was it that I had been praying and asking God for my "Mr. Right," but I was shooting him down at every turn only because he didn't meet the list. I realized that night that the list made no sense and that what I really needed was to throw it away. On the night that I was released at the stroke of midnight, my mama and sister were outside waiting for me. I couldn't wait to take a bath in my very own tub and sleep in my very own bed. The next morning when I woke up, I knew that I wanted to spend time with my babies.

So, I set out to take them to the mall shopping for shoes since Christmas time was rapidly approaching. My brother and I were in the mall shopping for shoes for the kids, and he called. I told him that I would call him whenever I made it in. I really wanted to be sure that I wasn't wasting any more of my time. That night before calling him back like I said that I would, I prayed, and I asked God if this is my husband, please reveal it to me. That night we ended up talking about family values and future goals.

As I listened to him talk, I kept saying; thank you to God because I knew that he was, in fact, my husband. In 2006, we were married on his birthday. The following year we welcomed a beautiful baby girl into our lives. She was the piece of the puzzle that we both had been missing all along. Although I had two kids already, this would be my husband's first child.

His parents first grandchild, everyone was elated to have her. That beautiful bundle of joy stole a piece of our hearts that we didn't even know was there. But if I was to believe that just because we were married that things would fall into place, I was wrong. For the first couple of years of our marriage we were more apart than we were ever together. When our daughter came into the world, I like so many before me thought that things would change because of a child I would be wrong again.

Adding children to the mix of an already complicated situation only makes things more complicated. We brought our baby home and by the following week my husband would once again run back home to his mama. I was inside of our apartment with three kids all while trying to heal from a C-section. I was so angry with him, and I vowed that I wasn't going to take him back. But just like before, it took him about a week to realize that he loved me and wanted to be with me.

It was embarrassing to have to ask my family for help with the kids, and then he just popped back up to pick up where he'd left off. Looking back over those times those cards was already in our hands they were there waiting to be played. Those first couple of years were long and hard because I wanted a "Mr. Right," but I wasn't a "Mrs. Right." To be honest, I didn't even know who I was, let alone learning about what a marriage looked like. I wanted my "Mr. Right" because I needed him to love me unconditionally.

I had never had it and I desperately wanted it, truth be told I would have done anything to get it because it meant that much to me. I thought that the love and affection that a man could give me would help to overcome the issues of my life. What I really needed to do was to love myself, and then I could offer love to someone else. I must admit that it was selfish of me to put such a heavy burden on anyone. We as women do this all the time, where we are trying to control the situation.

Whenever you find yourself doing this you are operating in what is called a "Jezebel" spirit. The spirit of Jezebel is a demonic spirit that ultimately seeks to control and rule over people. While I will not go into much detail about the great Jezebel spirit, I will say that she uses what she has, to control any situation. The Jezebel spirit uses fornication, premarital sex, alcohol, and drugs, etc. The great spirit of lust is a huge one that a lot of women know all too well about. Either because you have been a Jezebel, or you know someone that is a Jezebel.

Men, please don't get all judgmental and think that you guys don't tap into the realm of demonic forces. The Jezebel spirit could care less about the gender but more so the agenda. To get rid of this, you will most definitely need to get around someone powerful and filled with the Holy Spirit to cast this demon out. Afterward, you should refrain from doing the things that have caused the demon to come upon you in the first place.

• CHAPTER 7 •

SEEKING HEALING

AFTER JUST A SHORT WHILE after being married, the honeymoon stage was over. I began seeing my old ways reappearing again, and I started drinking again and doing drugs when my husband wasn't looking. Even though my husband loved me, I was a different person when I drank. My husband being as mild and meek as he was hated confrontation.

On the other hand, I handle confrontation very well. It was all I had ever known, so every chance I got, I was telling someone off. My voice was going to be heard loud and clear. And because I was a violent drunk, people hated being around me. I was the person that started the confrontation and finished it. Usually, both parties would be upset, and because I had so much pinned up anger on the inside of me, I wanted to fight all the time.

I began noticing that people would just let me say what I was going to say. They knew they weren't going to get anywhere with me anyway. This was something that I needed to change because as much as my family drove me crazy, I still loved them all. I wanted a relationship with them even if it didn't seem that way. My first thought was to stop drinking, but even when I was not drinking, I could still dice you to pieces with my tongue.

My husband had become increasingly angry with me and my mouth. For a very long time, it didn't faze me until I found out that he was having conversations with other women. I had to realize that even though I needed help through it all, he was still right there for me no matter what. One night for one of my cousin's birthday, she invited me to come and go out with her. I did, and the drinks kept coming in the club, by the time I made it home, I was beyond drunk.

My mama was on my mind and all I wanted to do was go to her house and jump on her. The pain was still there, but I didn't want it to be. This night would prove to me that a change was greatly needed if I wanted to be productive in life. My husband saw that I was much too intoxicated to be driving to my mama's house. He was only trying to keep me safe, but because of my drunken state, I didn't see it that way.

The next morning when I woke up, I heard the kids standing over me saying, "You think she dead?" I couldn't believe that I was putting my kids through these things. How could I stand before them as a mother and tell them right from wrong when I'm doing wrong? However, when I did get up to walk them outside to the bus stop, I couldn't help but notice that my house looked like I was robbed. I asked them what happened, and they said you were mad last night, and you were throwing things.

Their sleep had been interrupted because of me and my foolishness. I hated that they had to see me like that. I hated that I talked very explicitly around them. My husband and I would fuss and fight all the time, and to be honest, it was mostly my fault. In the beginning of our marriage, I was happy because I had found my "Mr. Right,' but then the enemy wanted that relationship too.

I can remember an instance where my husband and I were trying to be intimate. For some odd reason the way he manhandled me while taking off my clothes, triggered a memory inside of me that reminded me of the day I was leaned over a chair with my pants pulled down. In my mind he became my uncle, and I lashed out on him. It wasn't until that evening that he asked to talk to me. He wanted me to know that I called him by my uncle name. That's when I knew that I needed to heal. It had been more than a decade that this had happened to me.

The emotional aspect of it all still haunted me, and I was ready for it to be over. After all of that had happened in my life, the one thing that I had not done was go to God for my healing. I didn't know that it was going to be the only way to overcome the issues at hand. I had visited other church homes, and I still just was on the fence about it. I felt as though I just wasn't making the connection with the churches that I had been visiting.

I was just out in this big old world, wandering aimlessly without any guidance. So once again, I found myself praying to God for guidance. One day mama and I had gone to the hair store. Before we could even get out of the car good, mama spotted a family friend. Mama jumped out of the car and called out her name, and boy was she excited to see us.

I hadn't seen her in years, and even though I was happy to see her, I stayed quiet. I was on the fence about speaking to her because we hadn't seen each other in years. I didn't know her mindset after all those years had gone by. But she was the same loveable person that she was when we hung out together. I was also the same bitter black Jezebel spirit carrying woman that I was before just masking my true identity.

We immediately began catching up as she went on to tell me about her church. We exchanged phone numbers and kept in touch, but my friend was always inviting me to her church. While I was excited about seeing her, I wasn't excited about her persistently inviting me to her church. She and I eventually met up and did lunch one day just to catch up. I remember telling myself that I was just going to tell her that I hated when people invited me to their churches. I felt like the pressure of liking the church and becoming a member was too much for me.

That same week my husband and I argued something awful, and I knew that we needed God. However, I was still being stubborn about visiting any more churches. That weekend came, and mama and I went on a bus trip to the casino in Mississippi, just to getaway. The whole time I was there, I felt like I was being convicted of just being inside of a casino. On the ride back home, I made the decision that I would take my family with me to visit this church.

That way, if they didn't like it, then I wouldn't feel compelled to come back. The next day came, and me and the family got dressed to go and visit this church called "Lighthouse Christian Fellowship Center." The night before my husband said to me which he had said so many times before, "You can't let everyone pastor on you." We still decided the next morning to get up and get prepared to go to church. Once we got there the pastor was awesome and by the end of service, we would know why we were sent there.

As the service was coming to an end the Pastor did an altar call. Honestly, I never saw my husband get up and leave my side. I only saw him once he was standing in front of the church. The Pastor and the First Lady were laying hands on people young and old and they were being slain in the spirit and falling to the floor. My friend came and grabbed me and the kids and brought us up to the front of the church to be prayed for.

Seeing my kids as they went out in the spirit was amazing to me. It truly felt as if God was standing there at the altar when we left, the kids couldn't stop talking about it. That day we all agreed that we loved that church. Yet we were still on the fence about letting go of things that were going on in the world. Eventually, this church would become our church home.

I watched my family be healed, and I watched my kids blossom there. My husband never had any excuse about why he didn't want to go to church. Finally, I thought the pieces were all coming together but what about me? What was I to do with the pain, and the hurt that had become my security blanket? How do I serve God when I am hurting so badly?

I had so much going through my mind, and I couldn't let it go. However, when I would go, I always found myself crying out because I wanted to be rid of all the pain. I wanted to be normal and lead a productive life. It was a Friday the 13th of October in 2018, I had been throwing up for weeks at work, and was constantly in pain. However, because of the love for my job I continued to push myself to make it to work. On this Friday I left work early to go to the hospital, I figured that I would definitely be going home with some meds in tow for the pain.

I walked in and I told the doctor that I thought that it was a cyst on my ovaries that had burst. After looking over my bloodwork, he agreed with me that he thought that was the problem as well. However, he wanted to be sure that it was, in fact, the problem. He then turned around and sent me to have an ultrasound done. To our surprise, I was diagnosed with appendicitis; in other words, my appendix was about to burst.

As I sat there with my husband holding my hand as they tried to start an IV on me for the tenth time, I prayed. After I finished praying, they found a vein. They gave me some pain meds and told me that they would be admitting me into the hospital. At the time that this happened me and my mama had yet another argument and hadn't spoken to one another in days. She would be the first person that my husband thought to reach out to, to help get the kids.

I, on the other hand, reached out to my First Lady because I needed prayer. Before making the call, I thought about all of the people that get up in the morning leave to go to work and never make it back home again. That was me at the time; going under the knife is always scary, so I needed extra protection. My First Lady answered on the first ring, and I could tell that she was just getting home and trying to get her babies together. I informed her of what was going on with me, and we prayed together.

Shortly afterward, the doctor came in to tell me that he had the best surgeon coming to me in the next thirty minutes. If God was trying to get my attention, this was the day. I told my husband in the emergency room that we had to be at church every time the doors were opened. He agreed that was what was best for our family. Going into a church that was so very active was something brand new for me and my family.

Because of my insecurities, I hated "meet and greet." I just really didn't want people in my personal space. I can remember when it came to meet and greet time; I would always pretend that I was looking for something deep down in my purse. I just really wanted to come and get the word and go home. The bible tells us in Proverbs 27:17 "As iron sharpens iron, so a friend sharpens a friend."

If I wanted different, I was going to have to do something different. I realized that if I was to truly get my life on track I was going to have to get out of my own way. This church has so many different academies that there was something for everyone there. The hubby and I decided to take my friend up on the offer of attending the couple's academy. In this academy we were taught how to bring up touchy topics, how to let your partner off the hook and we even learned about our love languages.

After taking the love language test and finding out how we receive love was an eye-opening experience. From the test "The Five Love Languages.", we learned how to fill up each other's love tank by taking the time out to do something for your partner that will fill up their tanks. One of these topics really stood out for me, and that was letting each other off the hook. I learned that letting others off the hook would work not just in my marriage but in other relationships as well. There I was in this church meeting new people and allowing them to love on me.

I will say that the First Lady of the church was a huge hurdle for me to jump. I had a father figure that loved me, and that would do so much for me, so I found it easy to take to the Pastor. But I didn't really have a good relationship with my mama, and therefore it was hard for me to allow her to be a spiritual mother to me. Only because I didn't know what that looked like. I had never had a relationship with a spiritual mother before, and her telling me things kept me at bay with her.

I will honestly admit that I was in a state of rebellion, and I thought I was fine with it. If I thought that I was going to sit in this church and not learn how to do better, I was so wrong. They pushed me out of my comfort zone and into the safety zone. While I was trying to allow myself to build a relationship with my spiritual mother, I was having a horrible time with my own natural mother. The things that I needed from her I just wasn't getting, and I didn't know what to do about it.

I felt guilty that I was doing things with and for my spiritual mother and my own mama and I just fussed all the time. Even though decades had gone by, we still couldn't seem to get it together. Now that I have daughters, I felt that the relationship between my mother and I should be mended. I remember going to sit down and talk to my First Lady about how to start healing and mending my relationship with mama. She told me to pray about it and ask for peace, and clarity on how to approach the situation.

I thought that this was simple enough why hadn't I thought of that? While going through the different stages of trying to heal I was also trusting in my spiritual mother for spiritual guidance which was a huge step for me because it was hard to have another woman in my life trying to tell me what to do. I knew that I had to go through this because there were things that my First Lady had that I needed and one of those things was peace. Peace was something that I had always wanted but I felt as though it was unattainable for me. Even when it came to my First Lady, I was combative.

I was the girl that needed to know why, about everything. My First Lady was the person to tell me why whether I asked or not. I saw a lot of her in me but there were a lot of things that I had to correct in my life, if I ever wanted to stand in the arena next to her. Being submissive was one of them, from day one all I ever knew was to do for myself. So for me to allow a man to come in and take away my voice was manic to me.

However, I stayed the course with my husband because he stayed the course with me. Once I learned that being submissive was not about him controlling me, but me allowing him to lead in the marriage is God's design. I had to come to terms with me allowing my husband to get things wrong if that is what it took for him to lead. My life had been so stressful only because I was trying to do his job and my own. I was an emotional hot mess but when I started directing my kids to my husband things began to fall into place. My husband began communicating with me about the things that concerned the household.

I followed his lead as he took his rightful place and allowed God to cover him. As he followed God, he was instructed on how to lead us as a family. The pieces of our family puzzle began to come together. In one year, my husband received several raises and we were able to pay off the mortgage on our home. The biggest raise that he received was speaking in the Holy tongues.

He also began to experience the heavenly realm in such a way that some would call him a "glory junky." No matter where we are or what's going on, he occasionally slips off into the heavenly realm. As his submitted wife I am there by his side when others are looking and laughing to cover and protect the anointing that he has on his life. I recognize him going into that realm is not just for him but for my family as well. I make sure to have his back no matter what because if I haven't learned anything else, I've learned from all of this is that he is my "Mr. Right."

• CHAPTER 8 •

LEARNING TO FORGIVE

AFTER THEY REMOVED MY appendix, I knew that I needed to get to the root of the problem with my mama. Just as my First Lady suggested, I went to God about how to address the situation with mama. I heard Him loud and clear, saying to me talk to her. I thought to myself that I been doing that for years. However, I knew what I had to do to be able to forgive.

Forgiving was hard for me to do because my flesh wanted my uncle to pay. I wanted mama to pay for leaving me alone. I began thinking to myself about how I was going to get over this madness. Although I had no clue as to how I was going address this, I made sure to stay open for the opportunity. One night I decided that I would go over to mama's house because I hadn't been there in a while.

While I was there, my baby brother and I were in the room with my mama. The conversation presented itself for us to talk about our childhood. My brother was talking about how my daddy was never around for him and the things that he should have learned from him, but he didn't. Then I brought up the topic about mama leaving us and me being molested by our uncle. Not only were we left unattended, but mama never said that she even loved me.

She also never told me that she was sorry and that it hurt me more than anything. They both sat quietly as I expressed my sentiments through tears. The story was like a scab, and every time I went over it, I was opening it back up. This time my baby brother was there, and he said to mama, "Do you hear your daughter?" Her response was, "Yes, but what do you want me to do?"

He said mama, your daughter is telling you that you never said sorry and you never told her that you love her. Even though it was hard for her, she said she was sorry. She also told me that she didn't understand why I would think that she didn't love me. When mama told me that she was sorry that night, I knew that my healing had begun. I waited a very long time to hear her say those words to me.

That night when I was driving home, I gave God all the glory. I thanked Him so much for being there to bridge the gap between us. As I was praying and calling out to God, I heard him speaking, and He told me that I would have to forgive her. That night I was so happy that I could barely contain myself long enough to fall asleep. I just kept on praying and thanking God.

It was later that night that God continued to speak to me. He said everything that you could ever imagine on earth comes with an instruction manual except a baby. When a baby is born, the doctor removes the child from the mother's womb and places him or her in their mother's arms. From that point on, it would be trial and error, but love is what should bridge the gap between a parent and a child. When I woke, I knew that I was going to have to let my mama off the hook for leaving me. I was going to have let her off the hook about what had happened.

I was going to have to let her off the hook for her not telling me she loved me because mama thought that I didn't love her either. I was going to have to just get over the past and live for the future. Although it hurt me when she left me that day, I realized that she never intended for that to happen. All this time, I looked at her as the villain, but the truth is, she too was hurt. The evening she left, she was on her way to choir rehearsal, mama wanted to sing in the choir.

God had to show me that the enemy stole from both of us, not just me. As a mother, I couldn't even imagine leaving my kids and something like that happening to them. The enemy tried to tear a mother and daughter relationship apart. For many years he was able to succeed, but I was growing in Christ, and I was applying what I was learning. I realized that I had to take ownership of my actions and not hers.

I had to own up to how I treated her and how I fought with her. I had to forgive before I could be forgiven! Matthew 6:14-15 says, "If you forgive those who sin against you, your heavenly Father will forgive you. But if you refuse to forgive others, your Father will not forgive your sins." Colossians 3:13 says to "Make allowance for each other's faults and forgive anyone who offends you. Remember, the Lord forgave you, so you must forgive others."

For a very long time I did whatever I wanted to do, and now I was going to have to do what I needed to do. I had to start walking in the nine fruits of the spirits. Galatians 5:22-23 tells us, "but the Holy Spirit produces this kind of fruit in our lives: love, joy, peace, patience, kindness, goodness, faithfulness, gentleness, and self-control." All these things were what the enemy stole from me, and I was destined to get it back. My marriage, my kids, and my relationships were depending on it.

While mama and I had begun mending our relationship, there was someone else with whom I needed to make amends. One of my aunts, my daddy sister, wronged me when I was a little girl. This aunt was bold, she told it like it was and everyone thought that I reminded them of her. I loved my aunt, but I had never forgotten what she had done to me as a little girl. She stopped by our house one Saturday afternoon with her daughters.

They were all dressed in red tops, and blue bottoms, one of my cousins asked if I could go with them. My aunt told me that for me to go that I was going to need to wear a red top and blue bottom. She took us to the movies to see the movie "The Mighty Ducks." We enjoyed our time at the movie theater, but when she picked us up, I decided to tell her that my cousins were being bad. I was just joking with them, and I had no idea that she would get as mad as she did.

Once I told her that I was just playing with her, she said to me, "No, you're lying just like you lied on my brother." That hurt my feelings so badly, and I made a vow to myself that I wasn't going back over there with them anymore. As I got older, she and I became closer, but I had never brought that day back up to her. I thought about talking to her about it for a very long time. I just knew that she would take his side and that I wouldn't be able to mend this relationship.

When you have a relationship with the Father, He cares enough to work things out for you. With my aunt, I thought about writing her a letter but realized that I wouldn't be able to know her immediate reaction. Once again, I found myself in my First Lady's office crying because I wanted to be rid of all the pain. I told her about the issue that I had with my aunt. Her response to me was, what would it take for you to be alright? I needed to get it off my chest!

I needed her to understand where I was coming from. My First Lady told me that she would support me in any decision that I would make regarding this. She also told me that if my aunt didn't own up to it and apologize, I would still have to forgive her. I wrestled with what avenue to take to express to my aunt how she made me feel. I typed up a letter but didn't send it. I wrote a letter and still didn't send it.

Finally, one night she called just to talk to me, and I just came out and told her. I told her what she had done and what we had worn to the movies and what we saw. Her immediate response was that she didn't remember, but if she did, she wanted me to know that she was sorry. Another hurdle down I thought, I was so nervous about doing it, but God was there with me every step of the way. The next day at work, I received a phone call from her, and she was asking me was we good.

She was truly concerned about my feelings that day, I felt so much love from her. I was thrilled that I had gotten it off my chest, especially since she would pass away a few months after. All I could think about was that I was able to mend a relationship before it was too late. Although I was sad to see her go, I found solace in knowing that I made peace with her. I was also happy that we knew exactly where we stood with one another before her dying day.

Learning how to forgive is the best gift that you could give to yourself. Even with my uncle, I had to forgive him. Forgiving him helped me to sleep at night. Forgiving him enabled me to be able to forgive others so that I could, in turn, be forgiven. When I was able to say his name without crying is when I knew that the healing process had begun.

I had to forgive him because by not forgiving him means he still had dominion over me. I had to forgive him because it was hindering me from progressing in life. While I was on the brink of forgiveness, I cried out to God, and I asked Him, "Lord, why me?" He stated, if not you, then who? That night when I went to bed, I had a dream that I was back on that road, and the molestation had just happened.

God was showing me the answer to the question at hand. In the dream, we were standing in front of the house. My sister and brother were swinging without a care in the world. That's when God showed me, my sister. He said that it had to happen to you because if it had happened to her, it would have taken her out. That's when I knew that I needed to help others just like me because I didn't choose this I was chosen. If I had to do it all over again, I am not sure if I would change a thing. It was this very relationship that caused me to change.

• CHAPTER 9 •

WHAT YOU NEED TO KNOW ABOUT SEXUAL TRAUMA

SEXUAL ASSAULT/TRAUMA IS defined as any sexual contact or behavior that occurs without the consent of the victim. There are different types of sexual assault, which include: rape, fondling, or unwanted sexual touching, forcing a victim to perform sexual acts such as oral or anal sex. While these things are happening every day, the individuals need to know that it is never the victim's fault. As for the community, I want you to know that people who sexually assault children/young adults look just like you and me. They are usually in our families, churches, schools, and youth sports.

A sexual abuser can be of any relation and can come from any religion, race, and political background. Statistics show that ninety percent of children who are victims of abuse know their abuser. Only ten percent of sexually abused children are abused by a stranger. Once a child has been victimized, there are several different feelings that a survivor goes through after a sexual assault. It is powerless and loss of control, emotional numbness, disturbed sleep, flashbacks, denial, guilt and shame, low self-esteem, depression, mood changes, anxiety, suicide, and promiscuity.

Just like grief, there is no wrong or right way to get over a sexual assault. What the individual will need is time and lots of love. Following these steps can help to prevent your child from becoming a victim.

How to keep your children safe:

- **Show interest in their day to day lives.**

  Engage your child in healthy conversation. This way, they won't feel compelled to be engaged with others for whatever reason.

- **Get to know the people in your child's lives.**

  You should always spend time with these individuals and get to know them before you allow anyone to be alone with your child.

- **Choose caregivers carefully.**

  No matter who they are, this includes family members. Most of the time, it's the people that your child knows that commit the acts. Be very careful of who you leave your child with because a predator will wait for the right time and then pounce. Parents follow your first mind regarding your children.

- **Talk about the news and statistics.**

  Sexual assaults are happening every day, and people need to be aware of it. Making them aware will cause them to watch out for things that we don't see. It's time to start having those awkward conversations with your child. The more your child knows about these things, the better off they will be.

- **Know the warning signs.**

  Keep a watchful eye for any changes in your child, no matter big or small.

- **Encourage children to speak up.**

  This will come with you teaching them about healthy boundaries. Children never need to climb in the laps of others; a desire can come from just a single innocent touch.

- **Teach your child how to talk about their bodies.**

  Even at an early age, kids need to be taught about their bodies. This will help them to identify if they have ever been violated.

- **Be available.**

  Please always make time for your child; it is crucial. You, as a parent or guardian, should have an open line of communication with your child. When this line is closed off, you can subject your child to the predators that prey on kids.

- **Let them know that they won't get into trouble.**

  Predators are very manipulative, and they will try to convince your child that they might get into trouble for telling you. Kids do have a voice, and they need to be heard.

- **Give your child/children the chance to bring up the topic of sexual assault.**

  You never know, what you teach your child may help another child as well. By allowing them to bring up different topics about sexual assault, it allows them to problem-solve.

If you are a part of a family that has suffered through this, I will ask for your patience. Be patient even if the victim is acting out, grab them, and tell that you love them and that you are there. Keep the line of communication open with them and be ready and willing to talk even when you do not feel up to it. The victim will need time to heal and to figure out who they are. You also need to know that your presence will make a difference for the victim.

They will need to know that they are not alone, I cannot stress this enough. Knowing that they have someone to turn to could define their healing process. They will need someone there to help steer them in the right direction. Taking the time to love on them will show them that you care and that you are there if needed. If you do not know how to cope with this, I would ask that you seek help in learning how to deal with victims of sexual assault.

We didn't ask to become the victim of the heinous act of foolery. However, we are here! Victims speak your truth and take back what the enemy has tried to steal from you. Asking for help when you have been hurt is something that you are going to need. So, if you are having a bad day and you are reliving the demonic acts that have been forced upon you, trust and know that it's okay to say, "I'm having a bad day."

Talk out what is bothering you, the more that you suppress, the more the devil wins. It's alright to be angry, sad, or even mad but channel that to make a difference in someone else's life. Never push your support system away; you will need them for the rough times. Keep this in mind when you are going through different things. If you think that you do not have anyone on your side, try reaching out for help.

You may need to start participating in programs in your area to help with this. There is nothing wrong with seeking help when you are hurt, especially since it is not your fault. You did nothing to warrant this monstrous behavior that has been brought upon you. You, my dear, are a diamond in the rough. Polish yourself off and remain focused on your goals in life.

Focus on you and not what has happened to you. Seeking spiritual guidance will be greatly needed because God is the only one that has the tools that you will need to get through this. Get yourself in a faith-based church around individuals that you can trust. Psalm 27: 1 says, "The Lord is my light and my salvation, so why should I be afraid?" The Lord is my fortress, protecting me from danger, so why should I tremble?

When you are going through those rough patches in life, just know that the Bible says in Psalm 30: 5 "For His anger last only a moment, but His favor lasts a lifetime! Weeping may endure for a night, but joy comes in the morning." I have had to cry many nights because I too was a victim. Learning different scriptures helped me when it was just me and my tears.

When I discovered the scripture in Psalm 23:4 "Yea, though I walk through the valley of the shadow of death, I will fear no evil: for thou art with me; thy rod and thy staff they comfort me." This scripture tells me that no matter what, God promises to be there with me. This promise is the same for you; always remember that God is not a man that He should lie. Take Him at His Word, and He will see you through just as He has for me.

Made in the USA
Coppell, TX
08 February 2021

49915521R00059